Horns and Antlers

By Allan Fowler

Consultants

Linda Cornwell, Learning Resource Consultant,
Indiana Department of Education

Sharyn Fenwick, Elementary Science/Math Specialist,
Gustavus Adolphus College, St. Peter, Minnesota

Children's Press®
A Division of Grolier Publishing
New York   London   Hong Kong   Sydney
Danbury, Connecticut

Visit Children's Press® on the Internet at:
http://publishing.grolier.com

Designer: Herman Adler Design Group

Library of Congress Cataloging-in-Publication Data

Fowler, Allan.
    Horns and antlers / by Allan Fowler.
      p. cm. – (Rookie read-about science)
    Includes index.
    Summary: Examines the difference between horns and antlers, which
animals have which, what they are made of, and how they are used.
      ISBN 0-516-20806-3 (lib. bdg.)   0-516-26364-1 (pbk)
      1. Horns—Juvenile literature. 2. Antlers—Juvenile literature.
[1. Horns. 2. Antlers. 3. Animal weapons.] I. Title. II. Series.
QL942.F67   1998   97-23256
591.47—dc21   CIP
                                                          AC

How many animals can you name that have horns on their heads?

Sheep

Mountain goat

Texas longhorn

The cattle on farms have horns. Goats and sheep have horns, too.

So do antelope in Africa
and Asia.

Bighorn sheep

Among some kinds of
animals, only the males
have large horns.

Male and female bison
have the same size horns.

The horns of most animals grow out from their skull bones. The outside of a horn is made of something a lot like your fingernails and toenails.

A rhino's horns are not
made of bone. They are
made of fibers, like tightly
packed hairs.

The horns of this buffalo
curve back.

Other horns curl down,
or up, or down **and** up,
like the horns of this gnu.
A gnu (pronounced *new*)
is an African antelope.

Horns may curve inward, or outward, or form the letter "U"...

Dama gazelle

Greater kudu

. . . or look as if they
have been twisted into
a spiral.

13

The impala is a small
antelope with long horns.

The giraffe is a very tall
animal with short horns.

What about deer, moose, and elk? These animals don't have horns. Male deer, moose, and elk have antlers.

American elk

White-tailed deer

The females don't. But both
male and female caribou, or
reindeer, have antlers.

Antlers are made of bone and are covered with skin while growing. This skin feels soft, like velvet. When the antlers are fully grown, the animal scrapes the skin off.

Antlers grow prongs, which
are like the branches of trees.

While horns stay in place
all the animal's life, antlers
drop off every winter.

When the spring comes,
elk, moose, and deer grow
new, larger sets of antlers.

Moose are the largest animals
of the deer family. So they
grow the largest antlers.

Moose antlers grow up
to 6 feet (2 meters) wide,
with broad, flat surfaces
between the prongs.

Male deer, moose, or elk often fight each other to see which male, or bull, will be leader of the herd.

They go head to head, clashing their antlers loudly.

A very large set of antlers might be enough to scare away rivals— and attract females.

This poem will help
you remember the most
important difference
between horns and antlers.

The horns of an antelope,
cow, goat, or sheep
stay always in place.
A horn is to keep.

Black-faced sheep

Caribou

The antlers that crown
a moose, elk, or deer
are shed every winter,
and replaced the next year.

29

Words You Know

antlers

horns

prongs

skull

antelope

buffalo

caribou

deer

elk

giraffe

gnu

impala

moose

31

Index

About the Author

Allan Fowler is a freelance writer with a background in advertising. Born in New York, he now lives in Chicago and enjoys traveling.

Photo Credits